Flower Projects
for
Special Occasions

Flower Projects
for
Special Occasions

Joanna Sheen

PHOTOGRAPHY BY JACQUI HURST

MEREHURST

Published in 1994 by Merehurst Limited, Ferry House
51–57 Lacy Road, Putney, London SW15 1PR

Text copyright © Joanna Sheen 1994
Photography & illustrations copyright © Merehurst Limited 1994

ISBN 1 85391 246 8

A catalogue record of this book is available from the British Library.

Edited by **Heather Dewhurst**
Designed by **Lisa Tai**

Typeset by Servis Filmsetting Ltd, Manchester
Colour separation by Global Color, Malaysia
Printed in Italy by Rotolito Lombarda

Contents

Introduction

Flowers have always been part of special occasions. Whether it is a wedding reception, a Christmas dinner, a birthday party or a christening of a new baby, floral decorations add to the air of celebration. This book contains a wide range of inspirational flower projects to make, using fresh, dried and pressed flowers, which are suitable for celebrations throughout the year.

The first chapter contains many ideas for weddings, with projects ranging from a lavish lily garland to a charming miniature posy. The second chapter shows how to incorporate herbs into your arrangements for a more informal, country style, and includes baskets, wreaths and even an unusual herbal horseshoe. Christmas is the subject of the third chapter, which contains plenty of creative ideas for decorating your home, tree and even presents in a festive fashion. The final chapter contains ideas for floral gifts suitable for all occasions, from birthdays to Mother's Day.

I hope you are inspired by the ideas in this book and have fun arranging flowers for your own special occasions.

Chapter 1
Flowers for Celebrations

Flowers always play an important part in any celebration. Whether the occasion is a wedding or a birthday, some floral decorations will undoubtedly add to the success of the day.

If you are preparing flowers for a wedding, extra pairs of hands can often be a real help. It is a big undertaking to prepare wedding flowers and the saying 'many hands make light work' can certainly be true. Plan your time like an army manoeuvre and all will go well – leave it until the last minute and everything may well go wrong!

There are many occasions when you may want to have the expert help of a florist. But it is perfectly possible to do the flowers yourself if you have the time and the inclination. These projects should help you decide what you would like to make and show you how to create your decorations with the minimum of trouble.

Special occasions can be great fun and very hard work – but as much enjoyment can be derived from the preparations as the actual day!

Country flower basket

This delightful arrangement is ideal for an informal party or buffet. It brings the garden indoors and creates the effect of abundance. You can change the fruit or the colour of the flowers for different effects.

Country flower basket

An informal display of daisies, fruit and vegetables, this arrangement is fairly simple and yet rather different. The vegetables and fruit cannot be re-used as they have been wired, but they make a pleasant change from the more typical basket containing only flowers and foliage. You will need two bunches of white daisy spray, approximately 20 fresh runner beans, about 750g (1½lb) Brussels sprouts, 500g (1lb) kale and 6 to 8 green apples – although other alternatives could be substituted.

INGREDIENTS

4 terracotta or plastic flowerpots, 10cm (4in) in diameter

3 blocks of green florist's foam

Flowers, fruit and vegetables, see above

Clingfilm

A shallow basket, 45cm (18in) long

0.56mm (24 gauge) stub wires

Small, pointed wooden sticks

❧

1 Fill the flowerpots with pre-soaked florist's foam. Arrange the daisies in the pots to resemble growing plants. Ensure the foam is wet, but not so wet that the pots drip. Line the basket with clingfilm.

2 *Place the rest of the wet foam in the basket. Arrange the stems of kale in the foam as you would foliage. Place the pots of daisies into the arrangement. If they keep falling, insert a stub wire through the pots and into the foam in the basket to secure them.*

3 *Wire the sprouts by pushing the wire halfway through and then twisting the 'legs' of the wire together;*

bunch two or three together. Make small bundles of runner beans and push the sticks into the base of the apples. Add

groups of Brussels sprouts, beans and apples into each side of the arrangement.

Pew end

This decoration can be hung vertically, horizontally, or simply laid on a table. It has so many more uses other than the pew end it was originally designed to be! As the ingredients are all either dried or preserved, the arrangement will last for ages.

$\mathcal{P}$ew end

Having a piece of hardboard as a base is inexpensive and gives the arrangement many differing uses. Fit the hardboard with a 'D' ring picture hook to hang it vertically or 2 'D' rings with wire between to hang horizontally. If you intend to place the arrangement on a table, obviously no fixings should be added in case they scratch the table. You will need a small bunch of preserved oak and copper beech leaves, a bunch of orange carthamus, 3 large red hydrangea heads, 6 bell cups, a selection of artificial fruit and berries, some hazelnuts, dried red chillies and a bunch of red roses.

INGREDIENTS

Flowers, fruit and foliage,
see above

Piece of hardboard,
approximately
4cm × 15cm (18in × 6in)

Glue gun and glue

'D' rings as required

❧

1 Cut small sprays of copper beech and oak foliage and arrange them alternately around the edge of the hardboard, so *that you have a complete 'frill' of leaves around the hardboard and a bare centre. Glue the foliage into position.*

2 Glue individual carthamus heads between the leaves towards the edge of the arrangement. Add the hydrangea heads, broken down if necessary, and the bell cups, arranged so that they zigzag down the centre of the display. Fill the bell cups with hazelnuts, gluing them in individually.

3 Attach the bunches of berries and artificial fruits between the other ingredients, then add the chillies either singly or in small groups, depending on their size. Finally, add the red roses in clumps of three or five. Once the glue has dried, fit the pew end with 'D' rings, as required.

Welcome ring

This ring of flowers would look stunning as a welcoming arrangement for a summer party, barbecue or autumnal gathering. You will need a bunch of pale pink dried peonies (I have used 'Sarah Bernhardt' peonies), a bunch of 20 pink roses (these are called 'Souvenir'), a small bunch of pink gypsophila, a few ears of wheat and some preserved oak leaves.

INGREDIENTS

Glue gun and glue

Flowers and foliage, see above

Vine wreath, 25–30cm (10–12in) in diameter

3m (10ft) ribbon, 5cm (2in) wide

Silver rose wire

2m (2¼yd) chiffon ribbon, 4cm (1½in) wide

Scissors

❧

1 Glue the leaves around the wreath. Add in some ears of wheat. Using the wider ribbon, make a generous bow by wiring across a figure of eight (see diagram on page 131) and leave long tails to the bow. Attach this to the ring with wire and then make a smaller bow with the chiffon ribbon and attach that on top of the plain ribbon.

2 Glue on the peonies, having removed all but 2·5cm (1in) of their stems. Finally remove all the leaves from the roses and cut the stems down to about 5–7·5cm (2–3in). Then glue the roses into the arrangement, making sure that you use them evenly around the ring.

Wedding cake & Miniature posy

Although cake icing and sugarcraft are wonderful skills, not everyone has the ability to construct realistic flowers. This fresh flower decoration takes only a few minutes and looks wonderful. The miniature posy adds a special touch to a place setting or gift.

$\mathcal{W}$edding cake

There are very few who could undertake to decorate a wedding cake successfully with icing or sugarcraft, whereas decorating with flowers, although it involves a small amount of patience and a little bit of thought, should be beyond the skills of no one. The flowers can obviously be varied according to your colour scheme, but make sure you include something frothy like gypsophila as it lightens the design beautifully. Here I used a bunch of cream lilies, a bunch of peach roses, a little garden foliage, some gypsophila and a bunch of cream Singapore orchids.

INGREDIENTS

Wedding cake – in this case a 25cm (10in) base with a 17·5cm (7in) top tier

Flowers and foliage, see above

A reel of silver rose wire

A reel of green florist's tape

25cm (10in) cream ribbon

1 Make sure the cake boards are quite a bit bigger than the cakes to allow room for the flowers. A plain base with a minimal amount of decoration will suffice, but you can have more if you prefer. Before you start decorating the cake, put the pillars in position and mark the place so that you can reassemble the cake accurately if necessary. Make small flower bunches with either a lily or a rose in each, together with a few other ingredients. Wire them together then cover the wire and stems with green florist's tape. Each bunch should be no more than 7·5–10cm (3–4in) long.

2 *Once you have made up some bunches try arranging them against the bottom tier of the cake. They should all be roughly the same size or it becomes difficult to achieve the right effect. Lay one bunch over another, making sure that the wired ends are well covered by another flower. Place a spray at each end of the side of the cake and work towards the middle to camouflage the stems.*

3 *Make a larger bunch of flowers for the top of the cake, cover the stems with cream ribbon and tie in a* pretty bow. Now assemble the cake in its final position and place the flowers onto the cake. If necessary, you can cover one or two problem areas with individual flowers rather than entire bunches.

Miniature posy

This posy is quick and easy to make and would be a wonderful alternative to the more usual table decorations. The silver frill can be bought from craft or specialist floral outlets; alternatively you could spray a paper doily with silver or gold paint and use that. You will need 5 flowers from a bunch of spray carnations, a small amount of gypsophila, 7 ivy leaves and 7 small cones such as alder or larch.

INGREDIENTS

Flowers and foliage, see above

A reel of silver rose wire

A posy frill or sprayed doily

Ribbons, optional

Glue gun and glue

Green florist's tape, optional

1 Place a carnation in the centre and make a bunch with gypsophila and the other carnations. Wrap this firmly with wire, leaving a piece about 25cm (10in) long for finishing the posy, then cut the wire from the reel. It is important to use long-lasting flowers for the posy as they must look fresh throughout the celebration. Carnations are a good choice as they do not wilt too quickly.

2 *Place the ivy leaves around the edge of the posy and wrap the wire firmly around them. Other individual leaves could be substituted if ivy is not available. The posy could be finished at this point and the ivy leaves used as the frill if you prefer.*

3 *Push the posy stems through the frill or doily and tie some ribbons around if you wish. Using a hot glue gun, glue the small cones into position among the flowers. I think it looks pretty to leave the posy stems as they are; however, if you prefer, you can wrap them in green florist's tape.*

Rose & lily table centre

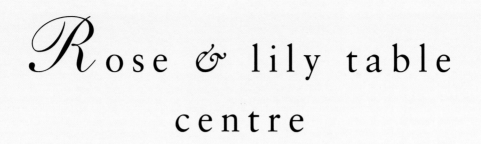

This small, cheerful arrangement would be ideal for the centre of a buffet table in a large function room. The terracotta base is fairly inexpensive and readily available from garden centres, while the flowers can be chosen according to those available in the garden at the time.

$\mathcal{R}$ose & lily table centre

This table decoration could be altered to suit any colour depending upon your choice for the occasion. The base is the saucer that is usually provided with a flowerpot. In this case it was bought separately for a very reasonable amount. The florist's foam should be well soaked so that the arrangement lasts as long as possible. Make sure the foliage has been cut from the garden the night before and soaked in a bucket overnight. You will need some greenery from the garden, a bunch of cream lilies and a bunch of peach roses.

Ingredients

Half-block of green florist's foam

Terracotta plant pot saucer, 12·5cm (5in) in diameter

Green floral sticky tape, optional

Flowers and foliage, see above

Scissors

1 Having soaked the foam well, cut it to fit tightly into the saucer. If you wish to secure it further you can use a green floral sticky tape around the foam and under the saucer. Insert some pieces of greenery into the foam to cover it well; a mixture of different varieties of foliage looks quite charming.

2 *Cut down the bunch of lilies, making several small sprays; the more open lilies can be used individually. Place them around the arrangement, putting the tighter buds towards the edge of the display and the more open flowers slightly further in towards the centre.*

3 *Finally add the peach roses to the arrangement. If you ensure they have had a long drink before you use them the table centre should last very well indeed. If you wanted to make a less expensive table centre, peachy/bronze chrysanthemums or peach spray carnations could be used instead of the roses.*

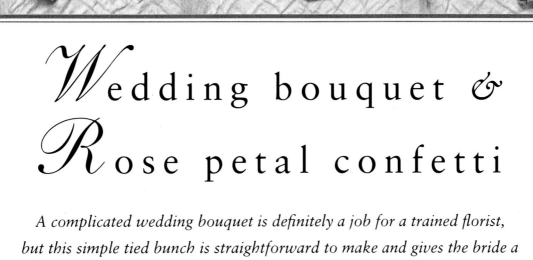

Wedding bouquet & Rose petal confetti

A complicated wedding bouquet is definitely a job for a trained florist, but this simple tied bunch is straightforward to make and gives the bride a beautiful armful of flowers to carry. Homemade confetti is far prettier than the coloured paper variety and very easy to make.

Wedding bouquet

This beautiful bouquet is fairly simple to make and, providing you have practised a few times before the day with some less expensive flowers or flowers from the garden, you should be able to master this project. It is important to use pretty ribbons; however, if the budget does not stretch to satin or wired ribbons then choose the most neutral colour, such as cream or white, so that the ribbon is not too obvious. An inexpensive paper ribbon would be fine. For the bouquet you will need 10 stems of cream lilies, some foliage such as pussy willow and phormium leaves, and some gypsophila.

INGREDIENTS

Flowers and foliage, see above

A reel of silver rose wire

3m (10ft) ribbon, 7·5cm (3in) wide

3m (10ft) ribbon, 5cm (2in) wide

3m (10ft) ribbon, 2·5cm (1in) wide

❧

1 *Make sure all the flowers and foliage have been well conditioned before you use them. Place some long pieces of pussy willow in a fan* *shape. Add in some more foliage and a big piece of gypsophila. Wire this together firmly to make a base for your bouquet.*

2 *Continue by adding stems of lilies into your bunch, wiring every few stems as you go. Keep the fan shape of the bunch and make sure the lilies are well distributed. Bring some of the flower heads well down the length of the bouquet. Check the bouquet from all angles; make sure you have used a reasonable amount of gypsophila as this lightens the bouquet. Add more greenery as you wish. Once you are satisfied with your bunch, wrap a piece of wire firmly around the bunch a few times to secure.*

3 *Take the widest ribbon and tie it around the bouquet to make a pretty bow with trailing ends. Then repeat with the middle width of ribbon, taking the ends across the wide bow and tying. This will give you a double bow. Then finish the bouquet with the narrowest ribbon, again tying the ends across the other two bows to give an even more splendid effect.*

Rose petal confetti

Dried rose petals have a fairly long life if you keep them warm and dark, so you could start planning and making your confetti several months before the wedding. Either garden roses or commercial roses can be used. Red roses keep their colour far better than any other rose but other varieties will all add to the blend of colours in the confetti. Make sure that you store them in a damp-proof box in a warm atmosphere.

INGREDIENTS

Bunches of roses

Airtight container

Rose essential oil, optional

❧

1 Hang the bunches of roses in a warm, dry place. Make sure each bunch is secured with an elastic band and not string, as the stems will shrink during the drying period. Alternatively, you can dry the rose petals individually by placing them on a cake rack in a warm room. It is best not to collect old rose petals that have fallen to the ground or you may find that most of them turn brown when they are dry as they may be too old.

34

2 *Once the bunch of roses seems completely dry, remove all the petals from the roses and store them in an airtight container. You may choose to keep the different colours separate or to mix them from the beginning. You will need the petals from quite a large number of roses to be able to shower a bride in a small cascade of confetti.*

3 *Once the petals are in the container, keep them well sealed and warm. As an extra touch you could add a drop or two of rose essential oil to intensify the scent but do not add too much or it will become totally overpowering. The dried petals should keep for several months.*

Circlet of flowers

Although a reasonable amount of wiring skill is needed for this project, with time and practice this can be achieved. It is important to use simple, robust flowers and to handle the flowers as gently, but firmly as possible.

Lily garland

A garland is a time-consuming project to make but the finished effect is lovely and can be used in many different ways. A doorway can be decorated with the garland above it or a gateway can have a garland twisted through it. This fresh garland could be hung outside or indoors – it would make a wonderful decoration for a fireplace or dresser for a summer celebration. You will need (depending upon the finished length you require) 10 stems of pink lilies, a bunch of white daisy spray, a bunch of pink daisy spray and plenty of garden foliage.

INGREDIENTS

2m (2¼yd) cord or twisted paper ribbon

A reel of silver wire

Flowers and foliage, see above

A reel of green florist's tape

Ribbons if desired, 1m (40in) per bow

ਦੈ

1 *Make a loop to hang the garland at each end of the cord or paper ribbon and wire it firmly. Make small sprays of the various ingredients. Wire each spray at the base. Then, using green florist's tape, wire them onto the cord or ribbon, starting at each end. Keep the bunches well spaced so that the garland does not become over-full.*

2 *When you reach the middle, overlap the stems as completely as possible and then cover any gaps by adding in individual flowers. Wire a large bow to the centre of the garland if desired. Ribbons can also be added in a similar fashion at either end if you wish.*

Presentation posy

Flowers are always a lovely way of saying thank you to someone. This posy is simple to make yet with its frill of handmade paper it is a little more unusual.

$\mathcal{P}$resentation posy

This posy could be made as a hostess gift or as a thank you for someone who has helped or spoken at a public occasion. The frill around the posy and the bow are both constructed from Japanese tissue paper. If you cannot obtain this paper, use ordinary tissue or handmade paper in a thin tissue version. Any of these makes a refreshing change from the more formal effect of cellophane. You will need a bunch of pink spray carnations and a bunch of pink alstroemeria. For the foliage I used telima leaves, picked in their autumn colouring, but you could substitute any other large individual leaves to go among the flowers.

INGREDIENTS

Flowers and foliage, see above

A reel of silver rose wire

Scissors

A sheet of Japanese tissue paper

Pin or glue

1 Make a small bunch with an open carnation in the centre, surrounded by alstroemeria and more carnations. Bind the stems with silver wire, keeping the binding to a minimum and in one position only. Make sure that the flowers have been in water for at least a few hours, preferably overnight, before using them.

2 Add more flowers and the telima leaves to the posy. There is no need to bind each ingredient in individually, simply wrap the wire around the stems once you have added three or four pieces. For a neater effect, keep the wire binding in the same position rather than travelling up and down the stems.

3 Cut a 7·5cm (3in) wide strip from the longest edge of the paper to act as the ribbon. Cut a large square from the remaining paper and fold it in half and then in quarters to make a triangle. Snip a small triangle from the end to make a hole. Slide the posy through this hole and fix the paper around the posy with a couple of twists of wire. Tie the 'ribbon' into a bow and fix it onto the posy with a large pin or some glue.

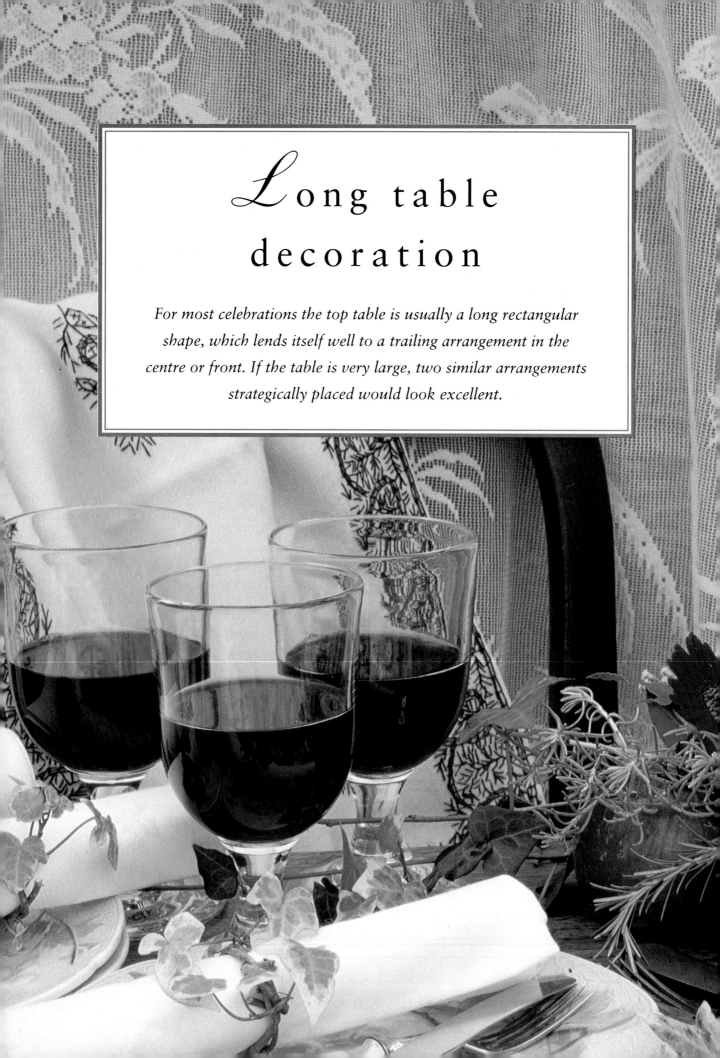

Long table decoration

For most celebrations the top table is usually a long rectangular shape, which lends itself well to a trailing arrangement in the centre or front. If the table is very large, two similar arrangements strategically placed would look excellent.

$\mathcal{L}$ong table decoration

The shape of this arrangement is ideal for a rectangular or oval table or, alternatively, for a sideboard or cupboard. It is important never to leave the room with the candles alight as the foliage could easily catch fire and spoil your celebrations. You will need a bunch of 9 small red gerbera, a few stems of solidaster and 20 or 30 small stems of assorted greenery. If possible, use some herbal foliage as this will add a subtle aroma to the arrangement.

INGREDIENTS

A block of green florist's foam

A dinner plate

Florist's tape

0.71mm (22 gauge) stub wire

Sticky tape

3 candles

Flowers and foliage, see above

Small, pointed wooden sticks

A selection of fruit

ᘉ

1 *Place the soaked foam onto the plate and fix it firmly to the plate with florist's tape. Take 9 pieces of wire, about 7·5–10cm (3–4in) long and bend them into the shape of* hairpins. *Tape three of these hairpins around each candle to act as supports, and push them into the foam. Cover the foam with the pieces of assorted greenery.*

2 *Insert the gerbera and small pieces of solidaster on all sides of the arrangement, making sure that the base of the candles and all the foam are well covered.*

3 *Push a wooden stick into each piece of fruit that you wish to use and add the fruit into the arrangement, making*

sure that it is firmly fixed into position. The fruit will deteriorate fairly rapidly as it has been damaged, but it

should last well through a festive weekend or few days.

CHAPTER 2

Herbs & Flowers

Herbs have played an important part in the everyday life of mankind for centuries – they can decorate, heal, soothe, and enhance the flavour of food, which has to make them one of the most valuable groups of plants that you could grow in your garden. If you are short of garden space many herbs can now be purchased fresh or still growing from supermarkets and delicatessens.

The beautiful soft greys and blues associated with herbs make them a joy to look at in the garden and a useful palette of colours to mix with other flowers and plants in decorations and arrangements. Herbs should never be considered too humble to play a part in celebrations and special occasions. The magic power of herbs has given them a position of respect throughout history and they were always part of any important occasion. Whether you use herbs in a small way, such as including some rosemary in a bridal bouquet, or give them a larger role, such as decorating tables with mixed herb arrangements, herbs always look attractive.

Basket of herbs

This rustic trug of herbs and daisies will last well as the flowers are in plenty of water and the herbs in pots. It would make a lovely display for a kitchen windowsill or table, and the herbs can then be used for cooking when needed.

$\mathcal{B}$asket of herbs

This is a very informal basket arrangement that would look charming on a kitchen table and can come in very useful when you need a sprig of basil or parsley. Herbs do not stay fresh in an arrangement for long, so this is the perfect answer – potted herbs together with flowers in separate containers of water. For this arrangement you will need a selection of abundant potted herbs – I have used 4 pots of basil, 3 pots of parsley, 2 pots of purple sage and some small white daisies.

INGREDIENTS

Herbs and flowers, see above

A rustic trug, approximately 35cm (14in) long

2 jam jars

Cut-flower food, optional

❧

1 Make sure the pots of basil have been well watered and place them in position in the trug or basket. Never use weak or weedy specimens as they will spoil the overall effect.

56

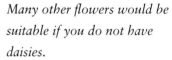

2 *Fill the jam jars with water and, if you wish, some cut-flower food. Place some sprays of small white daisies in the jars at varying heights. Add the daisies to the basket.*

Many other flowers would be suitable if you do not have daisies.

3 *Place the pots of parsley and sage in position to fill the basket. Try to choose herbs that contrast in colour as well as in leaf shape and texture, to give the best combination.*

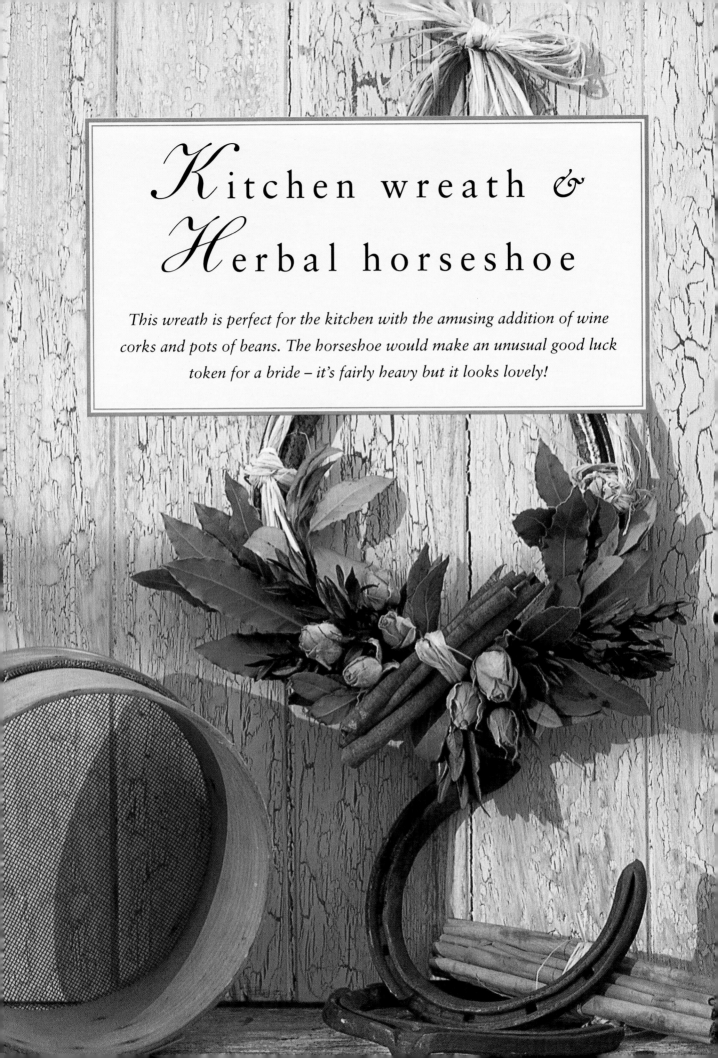

Kitchen wreath &
Herbal horseshoe

This wreath is perfect for the kitchen with the amusing addition of wine corks and pots of beans. The horseshoe would make an unusual good luck token for a bride – it's fairly heavy but it looks lovely!

Teacup of herbs

This lovely arrangement of fresh herbs and pansies can be made in a very short time, entirely from your garden. The finished project is quite charming and would delight anyone as a gift or as a decoration for a summer tea table. You will need a mixed selection of herbs, such as rosemary, rue (Jackman's Blue), grey sage and some small violas or a selection of pansies.

INGREDIENTS

Scissors

Small piece of green florist's foam

A cup and saucer

Flowers and herbs, see above

Fine rose wire, optional

Narrow purple ribbon, approximately 30cm (12in) long

1 Cut the foam so that it is fractionally larger than the diameter of the cup and press it in firmly. Soak the foam with water. Insert a selection of herbs into the foam all around the cup, making sure that you cover the foam completely.

2 Carefully add the violas to the arrangement. Their stalks are very soft so they do tend to break easily; if you find it impossible to push the stalks into the foam, gently wrap some fine rose wire around the stems to strengthen them. To complete the display, make a tiny bunch of the herbs and flowers used in the teacup, and tie it with the purple ribbon. This posy could then be laid on a matching saucer.

Topiary trees & Herbs in terracotta

These herbal topiary trees would make a lovely decoration for any room. The fresh herbs in terracotta are brightened by the addition of chilli peppers and kumquats.

$\mathcal{T}$opiary trees

These tiny topiary trees are really gorgeous and will make a very attractive centrepiece or windowsill decoration. Although they look impressive, they are relatively easy to make. Most herbs can be used but avoid the softer herbs such as basil that might not last so well. To make a topiary tree, you will need a large bunch of thyme and a cinnamon stick for each tree, plus the herb of your choice. Here I used curry plant foliage for the medium-sized tree and golden sage for the largest tree.

INGREDIENTS

A small terracotta container

2 pieces of green florist's foam

Cinnamon stick, approximately 15cm (6in) long

Knife

Herb of your choice

Ribbon or small flowers for decoration, optional

ﻬ

1 Fill the terracotta container with foam and soak well; cover any holes in the bottom of the container. Push the cinnamon stick into the foam and place the second piece of foam onto the stick. Cut the corners off this piece of foam to produce a spherical shape.

68

2 *Cover the base with a selection of greenery or the single herb used for the ball of the tree. Place pieces of herb at each side and at the top of the foam ball to give you the outer points of your circular shape.*

3 *Fill in the rest of the ball with small pieces of thyme, either placed singly or in small groups. Keep turning the tree as you are filling in the gaps so that the overall shape is as round as possible. Once the tree is complete, you could add further decoration, such as a ribbon or small flowerheads.*

Herbs in terracotta

Herbs make a delightful subject for an informal kitchen arrangement. Here herbs and some vegetables and fruit have been combined for an unusual combination. Any small vegetables could be substituted. The foliage and herbs can come from your garden or from a selection at the supermarket and florist's. You will need 7 or 8 pieces of bay, 7 large ivy leaves, and a bunch of rue (Jackman's Blue).

INGREDIENTS

Terracotta pot

Piece of green florist's foam

Small bundle of 0·71mm (22 gauge) florist's wires

1 Romanesco cauliflower

10 or more asparagus tips

7 kumquats

❧

1 Fill the terracotta pot with foam and soak well. Add the bay sprigs around the pot so that they almost cover the foam. Other medium-leaved greenery could be used instead, such as scented geranium leaves.

2 Add the ivy leaves to the pot. If they have strong stems you can place them straight into the foam; if the stems are too flexible to do this, strengthen them with some wire wrapped around the stem. The foam should be completely covered by now.

3 Add the rue throughout the arrangement. Then wire the pieces of cauliflower by pushing a wire halfway through the stalk and twisting the two ends together to make a wire stem. Wire the asparagus and kumquats in the same way. Place these ingredients into the arrangement to complete the design.

Bath sachets & Pot pourri

Bath sachets filled with herbs from the garden will give you a soothing, relaxing bath. The herbal pot pourri is also made with garden produce and is much prettier than commercial varieties.

Celebration basket

*This very special basket would make a
wonderful centrepiece for a special
occasion. Once made, it is very heavy and
should be moved as little as possible.*

Celebration basket

This magnificent arrangement is for a very special occasion and could be placed on the floor, on a side table or on the edge of a platform. Although this is a very large arrangement, items like bunches of grapes and artichokes can take up large amounts of the space and therefore save money on the flower content of the basket. To make this celebration basket you will need 2 bunches (10 stems) of stargazer lilies, a bunch of white spray carnations, 2 bunches of striped carnations, a bunch of white alstroemeria and 30 assorted stems of herbal and other greenery, including trails of ivy.

INGREDIENTS

Large, shallow basket, approximately 45cm (18in) long

Polythene

4 blocks of green florist's foam

Florist's tape

Foliage and flowers, see above

1 large bunch of purple grapes, 3 limes, 3 plums, 3 green apples, 3 globe artichoke heads, 3 purple and green kohlrabi or small purple-tinged turnips

Pointed wooden sticks, approximately 30cm (12in) long

&

1 Line the basket carefully with polythene and place the four well-soaked blocks of foam into position. Tape them firmly to the polythene so that they do not move about. Place the stems of assorted greenery in position, ensuring there are long flowing pieces of ivy on each side of the basket and a good mass of green foliage covering the foam. Keep the foliage reasonably low and well below the handle of the basket.

2 Add the lilies, with one in the centre to give height and one trailing on each side to blend with the ivy. Remember that the lilies will be tightly shut when you arrange them and they will only open a day or so later, so leave room for them to expand! Add the other flowers in groups, leaving room at the front for the grapes and a space at the side for the other fruit.

3 Impale each vegetable and each piece of fruit, except the grapes, on a stick. Arrange the fruit in the foam in groups. The grapes can either have a substantial wire wrapped around the stem and then planted in the foam, or the bunch can just be laid in the arrangement. It is important *to water the foam regularly as there will be many stems needing to take up water if the flowers are to survive for a reasonable length of time.*

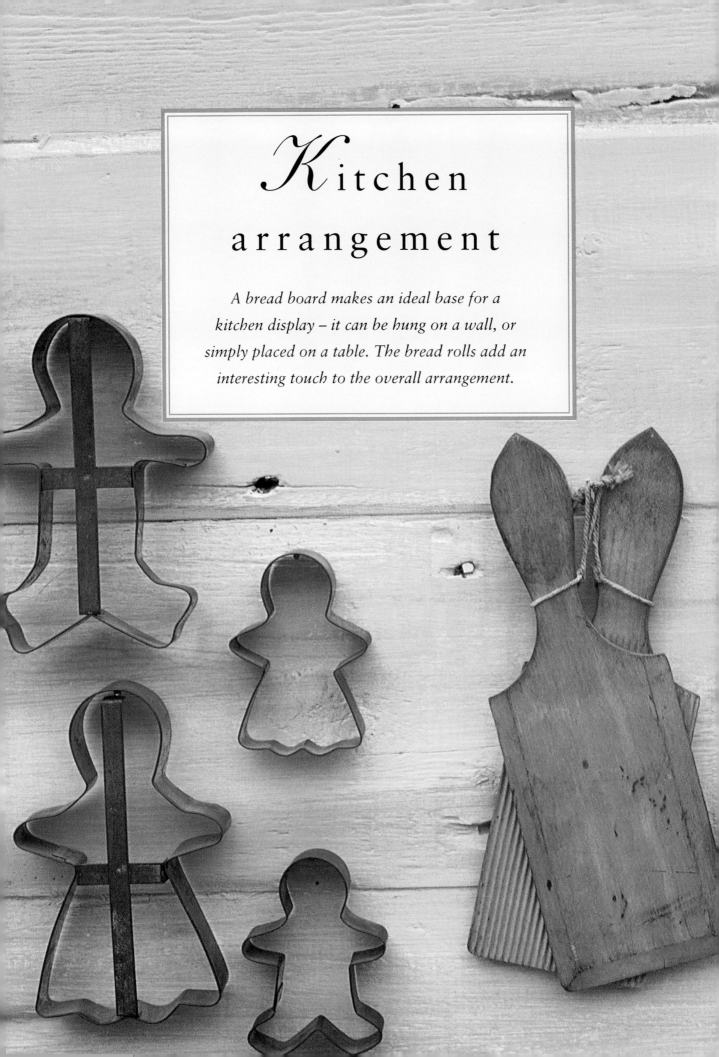

Kitchen
arrangement

A bread board makes an ideal base for a kitchen display – it can be hung on a wall, or simply placed on a table. The bread rolls add an interesting touch to the overall arrangement.

Kitchen arrangement

This decorated bread board hangs on my wooden cooker hood and has looked very attractive for many years. It is important to give the finished arrangement a good coat of varnish to help it survive the grease and dust in the kitchen. The varnish makes it much easier to keep clean. The bread rolls should be dried in a slow oven and then heavily varnished. You will need some marjoram, bay leaves and wheat.

INGREDIENTS

Silver rose wire

Herbs and foliage, see above

A bread board, approximately 25cm (10in) in diameter, with 'D' ring hanger

6 cinnamon sticks

Glue gun and glue

4 assorted bread rolls

2 terracotta ornaments or flowerpots

6 slices each of dried orange and dried green grapefruit

Wood spray varnish

1 Wire the ears of wheat into small clumps of three ears. Lay them onto the board and move them around until you are happy with their places. Then place the cinnamon sticks in position so that they cover the wheat stems. Glue them down firmly.

84

2 *Glue in the bread rolls and terracotta ornaments. If you cannot find similar little jugs, terracotta pots would look fine. Glue in the marjoram to fill any gaps.*

3 *Add the fruit slices, if necessary cutting them in half so that they do not protrude too far. Then fill in any gaps with bay leaves. Finally, give the arrangement a good spray of wood varnish – outside, because of the fumes.*

CHAPTER 3

Flowers for Christmas

Christmas is not only a time for families and celebrations, but also for flowers and decorations. Whether you are spending Christmas in a small apartment or a big family house, there is always a place to hang a decoration or two.

Homemade Christmas gifts are very precious and special wrapping adds to the overall effect. In this chapter there are ideas for packaging parcels and decorating crackers, and making all sorts of arrangements from holly rings to topiary trees, all of which will add extra sparkle.

As Christmas is a time for sharing and joining in, many of these projects could by made by younger flower arrangers, but with plenty of adult supervision, of course!

So whether you are planning your floral decorations for Christmas well in advance or looking through for last-minute ideas, I hope you enjoy the projects and are inspired to move on to other creative ideas and designs.

Holly & ivy ring

Christmas wreaths and rings are a welcome sight on doors during the festive season. This idea is a little different with the golden eggs adding an extra sparkle. The basic ring can be made at home or you can use a commercial wreath as the base.

Holly & ivy ring

A traditional holly ring always looks pretty at Christmas and will last well against the elements. This combination of holly and ivy will last for quite some time and the feature of the twigs and gilded eggs adds an unusual twist to a very popular Christmas decoration. You will need plenty of sprays of holly and some very long trails of ivy. The eggs are emptied of their contents by piercing them at each end with a large needle, waggling the needle inside the egg to break down the white and yolk, and then blowing gently through one end. Once the eggs are empty, rinse the shells well with clean water to make sure all the contents have been removed and leave them to drain overnight.

INGREDIENTS

Glue gun and glue

Holly and ivy, see above

A twiggy ring, 30cm (12in) in diameter

A bundle of lichen-covered twigs

5 eggs

Gold spray paint

1 *Glue the sprays of holly all around the ring, covering it evenly but not so densely that you cannot see the twiggy ring underneath. Both plain holly and variegated holly look very attractive, or you could use a mixture of them both. If you cannot find any holly, any other evergreen leaf could be substituted.*

2 *Wind the trails of ivy around the ring, bending them through the holly leaves and in and out of the centre of the ring. This will hold them securely enough, but you could glue each end to keep them in a particular position. Make sure the ivy has been given a long drink in water before you use it to help the ring stay fresh for as long as possible.*

3 *Glue the lichen-covered twigs in position. You could either add the twigs to a central point or offset to one side. Spray the eggs with gold paint and, when dry, glue them to the ring cluster. Place a few ivy leaves between each of the eggs to complete the festive decoration.*

Fireside basket

This unusual display of bayleaf balls and fresh orange pomanders adds a lovely spicy aroma to the room. The arrangement also looks attractive when dried. Extra essential oil can be rubbed into the balls or pomanders to strengthen the scent.

Fireside basket

Whether you have a real log fire or just a radiator, the warmth will help release the lovely natural perfume of these pomanders. The bay leaf balls are a little fiddly to make but last well and can be enjoyed for ages after they have been made. The orange pomanders can be enjoyed while they are drying and then arranged with fruit or as a decoration on their own. You will need a carrier bag full of fresh bay leaves – more than you might think you need, as many may well be damaged. The oranges also take quite a few cloves so it is best to buy a large pack or two from a herb supplier.

INGREDIENTS

Bay leaves

0·71mm (22 gauge) stub wires

Assorted foam balls, 7cm (2¾in) and 9cm (3¼in) in diameter

Glue

Cloves

Oranges

ॐ

1 Sort out the bay leaves, discarding any that are damaged. Cut the wire into approximately 5cm (2in) lengths and bend each in half to make a 'hairpin'. Use these hairpins to pin the bay leaves onto each foam ball, so the entire surface is covered. The patterns you create are up to you – you can start from the top or middle, so long as the leaves overlap each time.

2 *Continue to cover the ball until the foam is completely covered. Cover the joins between the rows of leaves by changing direction and pinning leaves across each other. The last few leaves can be glued on with a small amount of glue to prevent the wires being seen.*

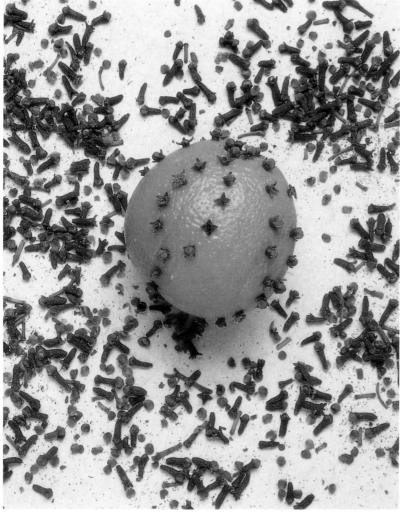

3 *Tip the cloves onto a flat surface and press them one by one into the skin of each orange. You can make many different patterns with the cloves – swirls and stripes or patches, circles and sections. Place the decorated oranges into the basket together with the bay leaf balls.*

Christmas pot pourri

Memories of Christmas are as much about scents and aromas as they are of tastes and sights. Spiced wine mulling in a large pan, aromatic cinnamon and tangy oranges – all of these bring Christmas memories to mind. A festive pot pourri can encapsulate many of these fragrances. For this recipe, you will need 10 slices of dried orange, 10 cinnamon sticks, 10 nutmegs, a cup each of dried marigold flowers, dried green leaves, rose hips and costus flowers or small pine cones. For the essential oils, I used a mixture of cinnamon, ginger and orange.

INGREDIENTS

Dried ingredients, see above

Bowl and metal spoon

15g (½oz) orris root

10ml (2 tsp) essential oils of your choice

Large plastic bag and elastic band

Container for pot pourri

❧

1 Assemble all the ingredients; put aside some orange slices and cinnamon sticks to decorate the top, but cut or break the rest. Place the ingredients in a bowl, add the orris root and essential oils, and mix well with a metal spoon.

2 Tip the mixture into a large plastic bag and shake well. Secure the top with an elastic band and store for at least a week for the perfumes to mature and blend. Then tip the pot pourri into the container and decorate the top with the reserved orange slices and cinnamon sticks.

Floral parcels & Decorated crackers

Beautifully gift-wrapped parcels need not take hours to do or cost a lot. These floral giftwrap ideas are inexpensive and make a parcel really special. Christmas crackers, too, can look really sumptuous, simply by adding extra decorations.

𝒴uletide table centre

All that does not glitter can easily be sprayed gold! Gold materials look very effective in Christmas displays and when combined together, as in this arrangement, they make an excellent focal point.

*Y*uletide table centre

The main thing to aim for with a Christmas table centre is a bright, cheerful centrepiece that will add some festive sparkle. The table is always crowded with glasses, plates and other dishes so it is best to keep any floral decorations fairly compact. Most of the items in this arrangement have been sprayed with gold paint which adds a special glow to the display. You will need some preserved oak foliage, 5 cardoon heads, 15 gilded pine cones, 15 natural walnuts and 9 golden mushrooms.

INGREDIENTS

Glue

A plastic 'frog' fixing

*Oval cork base,
25cm × 20cm (10in × 8in)*

*Half-block of dried flower
foam*

Secateurs

*0·71mm (22 gauge) stub
wires*

*1m (40in) bronze chiffon
ribbon*

1 Glue the green frog fixing to the cork base. Once it is firmly fixed in position, impale the dried flower foam over the prongs of the frog. Cover the surface of the foam with sprays of gold oak leaves, keeping the oval shape of the arrangement.

If the foam seems too high, cut some off the top with a knife to make the arrangement slightly shallower.

2 Push the gilded cardoon heads into the foam, making sure they are well spaced and not too close together. You will need very short stem lengths on these or they will stick out too far. Wire up the pine cones by winding some wire around the base petals of the cone, then bend down the wire and use as a stem. Add them to the arrangement.

3 Fill in the arrangement with wired walnuts (if you prefer you could glue them into position) and wired golden mushrooms. Take some chiffon ribbon and make a few loops, holding the base of the loops between your thumb and forefinger. Then wrap wire around the base to secure (see diagram on page 131), bend down the wire and press into the arrangement. Place loops on both sides of the table centre.

Traditional arrangement

This very traditional combination of poinsettias, holly and conifer sprigs always looks attractive at Christmas time. If you prefer a larger version, the poinsettias could be used in their pots rather than in foam.

Traditional arrangement

Although it is fun to make modern or unusual flower arrangements and come up with new ideas as often as possible, it is also very satisfying to make a really traditional Christmas arrangement. This particular idea reminds me of many Christmas cards I have received over the years and I like the comforting feel of an arrangement one almost seems to recognize! For the foliage, I used a mixture of blue spruce and variegated holly, about 9 stems of each, and 3 large red poinsettia flowers.

INGREDIENTS

Half-block of fresh flower foam

Long shallow container, approximately 20cm × 10cm (8in × 4in)

3 candle holders

3 ivory candles

Foliage and flowers, see above

2m (80in) red ribbon, 2·5cm (1in) wide

2 × 0·71mm (22 gauge) stub wires

ॐ

1 *Soak the foam in water until it is saturated. Wedge the foam into the container. Press the three candle holders into the foam wherever you would like them. Trim two of the candles so that they are all differing heights. Fix the candles into the candle holders. Place 15cm (6in) long sprays of both foliages into the arrangement.*

2 *Cut the poinsettia stems to a suitable length and add them to the arrangement. Keep them spaced well apart so that they do not look too crowded.*

3 *Make two wired bows from the ribbon (see page 131) and place them at either side of the arrangement so that the display can be viewed from both sides. Take care never to leave the arrangement unattended when the candles are alight as indoor bonfires are most unwelcome!*

Topiary tree & Indoor wreath

The little apple and cranberry topiary tree is a pretty and unusual decoration which is simple enough for children to make. The wreath is an idea for indoors as the ingredients are definitely not weather-proof.

Festive garland

*This luxurious spruce garland can be made at home
for a fairly reasonable price. Although it takes a little
while to make, it does look wonderful!*

Festive garland

Spruce is a very attractive foliage to use at Christmas and it has the added benefit of lasting very well. It will not drop like some conifers or traditional Christmas trees – it just dries and turns a greyish-blue instead of bluish-green. It will take a reasonable amount of spruce to make this garland – about 50 sprigs to make a 1·5m (62in) garland. It is hard to be accurate about the exact number required as it depends on the quality and density of the spruce.

INGREDIENTS

1·8m (6ft) twisted paper ribbon

A reel of binding wire

Spruce, see above

1m (40in) wired ribbon, 6·5–7·5cm (2½–3in) wide

Glue gun and glue

Assortment of gilded poppy heads, cinnamon sticks, walnuts, dried orange slices, pine cones and gilded lotus heads

Spray gloss varnish

❧

1 Bend some twisted paper ribbon over at both ends and wire firmly to make a hanging loop at each end of the garland. Twist a small piece of wire in the middle of the garland to remind you where the centre is. Starting from one end, place a 10cm (4in) sprig of spruce over the loop and wire it onto the twisted paper ribbon. Keep adding pieces of spruce, fanning them out so the garland is fairly flat rather than chunky. Continue until you reach the marked middle point, then turn the garland around and start from the other end.

2 *Once you reach the middle point, cut some smaller pieces of spruce and place them at right angles to the ribbon and wire on to fill the gap in the middle. Use plenty of wire as it is more important to have a secure garland than a neat one, and the glued-on bits and pieces will cover most wiring problems. Make a large bow with the ribbon (see page 131) and attach it to the centre with glue.*

3 *Glue on all the bits and pieces you have chosen. Place larger pieces like the lotus heads on first, and the cinnamon sticks through the centre of the bow and at intervals along the garland. Once you have all your nuts and cones glued on, give them a coat of spray gloss varnish as this will highlight their colours and give the nuts in particular an attractive shine.*

Christmas tree decorations

We all have many beloved family tree decorations that have been around for years – some may be very special as they were made by the children. Although there are always new, different and exciting commercially-made tree decorations on the market, these homemade decorations are a little bit different, and something perhaps the whole family could make together a couple of days before Christmas. You will need some sea lavender, solidago, spray carnation, 1 or 2 roses, and any fresh foliage from the garden.

INGREDIENTS

Gold wire or cord

Terracotta flowerpots, 2·5cm (1in) in diameter

Fresh flower foam

Flowers and foliage, see above

Silver rose wire

Cellophane

Curling ribbon

❧

1 Thread two loops of gold wire or cord through the hole in the base of each flowerpot to act as hanging loops for the decoration. Fill the pots with foam that has first been *soaked in water and make a miniature arrangement with foliage, sea lavender and solidago. The ingredients can be altered according to what is available.*

2 Make some small bunches of carnations or roses with sea lavender or solidago, and wire into a small posy. Add a wrapping of cellophane and secure with curling ribbon, adding a loop to hang them from the tree.

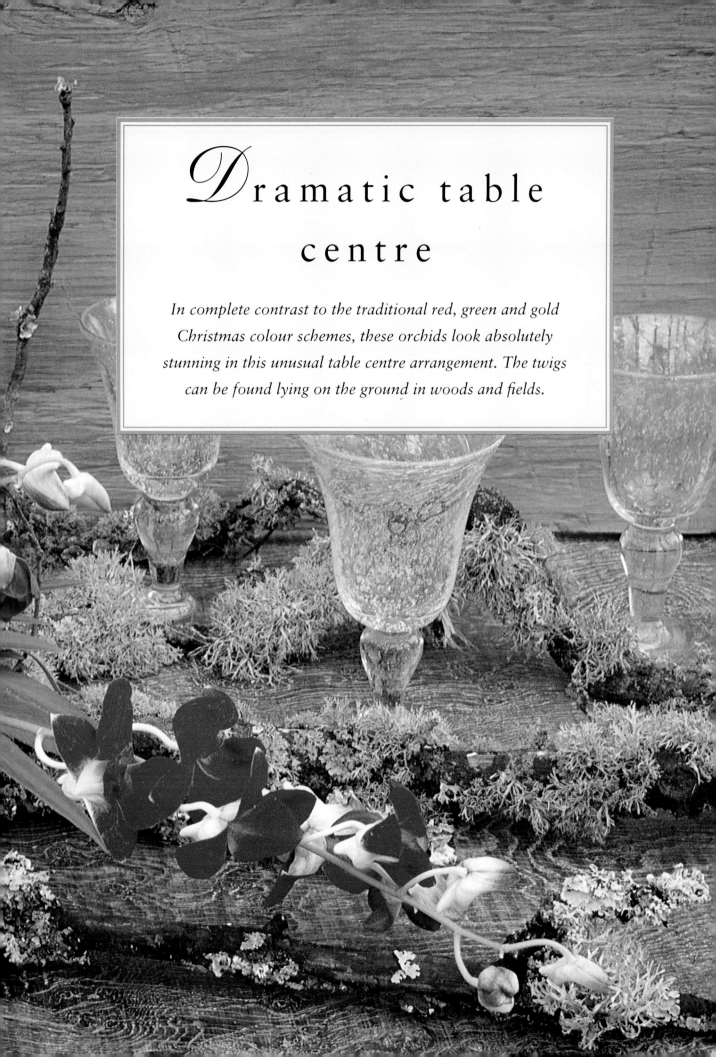

$\mathcal{D}$ramatic table centre

In complete contrast to the traditional red, green and gold Christmas colour schemes, these orchids look absolutely stunning in this unusual table centre arrangement. The twigs can be found lying on the ground in woods and fields.

Dramatic table centre

The colouring of this arrangement is by no means traditional, but it is certainly dramatic and would be ideal for a New Year's Eve celebration. Although it looks very impressive, the actual arrangement is very easy and will only take a short while to make. The list of ingredients is quite short – you will need 2 small bunches of mauve Singapore orchids, a selection of lichen-covered twigs and some hellebore leaves.

INGREDIENTS

Fresh flower foam

Small baking tin or other container, approximately 15cm (6in) wide

Flowers and twigs, see above

1 Soak the foam in water until it is saturated and fill the tin with it. Lay the twigs in position if you are arranging the flowers in situ; if not, then lay them on the table and add the container with flowers after Step 3.

2 Insert the hellebore leaves into the foam, making the arrangement long or round, depending on the shape of your table. If you cannot obtain hellebore leaves, any other large, dark leaves would be suitable.

3 Next add the sprays of Singapore orchids. If they are very long, break them in half and add both halves towards *the centre of the display. These orchids are also readily available in other colours so the arrangement could be* *varied simply by the substitution of cream or peach orchids, for instance.*

Preparing for Christmas

Many of the items used in these projects can be bought all year round, but some may need a little advance preparation. Think ahead during the summer days and harvest flowers and seed heads for drying at the right time, and store them away in a warm, dark place.

PLANNING AHEAD

The projects using dried or preserved items can be made in advance and stored. Make sure, however, that you pack them away carefully – preferably in the dark. It is all too easy for another member of the family to damage something that has been carelessly left in the spare room, unless they are all warned in advance!

Fresh ingredients such as blue spruce and holly can be cut a little while before Christmas, but make sure they are kept cool and damp. Spruce lasts very well if it is kept outside with the occasional rain shower keeping it watered!

SPRAYING WITH GOLD AND SILVER PAINT

Spraying plant material, such as dried seed heads, with gold or silver paint can add a truly festive touch to arrangements. There is no need to stop at seed heads or other dried flower bits and pieces when you are thinking of things to spray. Artificial fruit looks wonderful with a coat of gold or silver – and that includes the cheapest, most unrealistic plastic specimens that you never thought would be useful at all. Bargain baskets and containers that were a hideous colour look quite transformed when they are given a liberal coating of gold or copper metallic spray.

Spraying with gold paint can be a very messy affair. The easiest way is to lay the items you want to spray in a large shallow fruit box – the sort used by supermarkets. Spray one side and then once they have dried off a little, turn them over and spray the other. If you decide to take items out in the garden to spray, to take care to protect your hands and shoes. The spray drifts quite a lot and I have ruined a couple of pairs of shoes with the addition of gold paint speckles!

MAKING A WREATH BASE

As a change from using shop-bought wreath bases, you might consider making your own wreaths or rings. You could try using lengths of vine or clematis stems, but for a really sturdy wreath I have found the trimmings from a willow tree the most successful material.

Make up a board with nails placed in the pattern as shown in the diagram opposite. The size of the board will depend on the finished size you want your wreath to be. Wind the stems in and out of the nails on the board making a good circular shape, easing each piece around the bends. Continue with plenty of stems until you have a sturdy wreath. As the depth of the ring increases, try to wind some of the stems through the others to make the wreath even more secure. Once you feel that you have a ring of the shape and size that you are happy with, slide some lengths of wire under the ring in various places around the circle and knot or twist the wire so that it holds the depth of the ring in shape.

Leave your wreath on the board to dry in a really warm place, such as a boiler cupboard, until the stems have dried completely. This will take varying amounts of time depending on the variety of plant material used and the dampness.

MAKING A BOW

Bows always feature largely in Christmas arrangements and packaging and making a wired bow is much easier than it looks and is a technique worth trying. The diagram on the right illustrates where the wire should be tied. Take a length of ribbon and wrap it around like wrapping a shawl around your shoulders. Gather up the middle, making a bow and tails and bind the middle with some wire. The wire can be hidden by tying a small piece of ribbon around it or by covering it with flowers or other decorations.

The overall effect at Christmas should be one of abundance and cheerfulness. So don't worry too much about the technical side of your ideas or arrangements, just have fun, rope as many of the family in as possible and make the house look happy and friendly.

Collect an assortment of useful Christmas decorations for your arrangements (above). Make a wired bow in two ways, and a board for a wreath base (below).

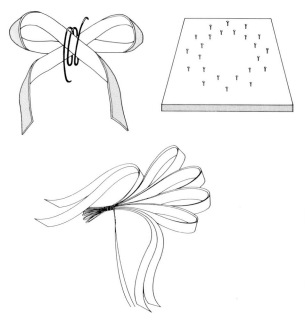

CHAPTER 4

Floral Gifts

Flowers make wonderful gifts for all age groups, and for both sexes. Although traditionally flowers have been given as gifts to women, there are many male gardeners who would love to receive a gift of plants or a bunch of flowers.

A gift made with dried flowers has the bonus of early preparation – you can make Christmas or birthday offerings well in advance, provided that they are kept fairly warm and dark to prevent any absorption of moisture or colour loss. If you plan to make quite a number of your own Christmas presents, any that can be made and tucked away are an invaluable help to finishing everything on time! Although some of the projects are aimed for specific occasions, with a small change here and there they can easily be adapted to suit many others. If you have a good collection of basic flower arranging items such as foam, containers, wires and ribbons, then a present can be made very quickly should the need arise.

Table centre

A combination of fresh and preserved material gives this table centre an unusual look, which can be changed very easily by adding new fresh flowers to the small displays on each side of the basket. The centre can be filled with chocolates, nuts or fruit.

Photo frame & Dressing table posy

A photo frame is always a popular gift and the addition of a small flower decoration makes this frame even more attractive. The posy would look charming in any bedroom, whether the lady in question is nine or ninety!

$\mathcal{P}$hoto frame

A plain photograph frame can be enlivened by the addition of a small flower arrangement and the flowers changed time and time again. The small container used in this example was a brown aerosol lid but any other small and moderately inconspicuous container would be suitable. If the item you wish to use is a lighter colour than the frame then I would suggest painting it black or dark brown to help camouflage its presence. You will need only a small amount of flowers and foliage – if you do not have a garden then small pieces of house plant foliage would be a possibility. This example uses a few hellebore leaves, three pieces of conifer, a few strands of ivy, some larger ivy leaves and a spray of Singapore orchids.

INGREDIENTS

Small piece of green florist's foam

1 dark-coloured plastic container

Glue

Plain, wide photograph frame, 25cm × 20cm (10in × 8in)

Flowers and foliage, see above

ã

1 Soak the green foam in water. Fill the container with foam and, using a strong glue such as a hot glue gun, attach the container to the bottom of the frame. Leave until completely dry.

140

2 *Arrange the pieces of foliage into the foam, covering both the foam and plastic container as much as possible. Place some taller pieces of ivy coming up the frame and others trailing to soften the arrangement. Any combination of greenery could be used.*

3 *Cut the spray of orchids into 2 or 3 pieces and add them into the arrangement. Make sure the foam is kept wet but not overwatered or it may leak onto the surface on which it is standing.*

$\mathcal{D}$ressing table posy

Although posies and bouquets are perhaps thought of in connection with weddings and celebrations, they are also very pretty ornaments to have displayed around the house. This pink and cream posy would look charming on a dressing table or indeed elsewhere in the home. If you are unable to find a commercial posy holder, a similar posy could be made by wiring all the ingredients together. To make this posy, you will need a small bunch of eucalyptus (fairly small-leafed variety), a bunch of dark pink larkspur, a bunch of dark pink roses, and about 20 wired cream helichrysum.

INGREDIENTS

A posy holder

A frill to fit posy holder

Glue

Flowers and foliage, see above

ॐ

1 *Attach the frill to the posy holder with glue. Break down the eucalyptus into pieces of a suitable size. Arrange them evenly across the foam ball in* *the centre of the posy holder. Use as much eucalyptus as necessary to give a good covering to act as a base for the posy arrangement.*

2 *Cut the pink larkspur into small pieces and push them into the foam so that they are evenly spaced throughout the arrangement. Do not make them too long or the posy will look straggly and untidy. Make sure the lace frill is still perfectly visible.*

3 *Cut the rose stems and helichrysum wires to the correct length and place the flowers into the posy. Scatter them evenly throughout the arrangement. It is a good idea to plan where they will go before inserting them in the foam to ensure that you do not have too many cream or pink flowers in any one part of the posy.*

143

Get well soon basket

Nothing lifts a patient's spirits more than beautiful fresh flowers at the bedside. These fresh colours are a cheery reminder of spring, but an equally beautiful arrangement can be made at other times of the year using alternative flowers.

Get well soon basket

If you are feeling at a low ebb, recovering from an illness or just a bad cold, nothing lifts the spirits more than some pretty fresh flowers to brighten the room. Spring flowers are particularly cheering and lightly scented flowers help to perfume a bedroom or hospital ward but all flowers have a special magic! Make sure that you do not make too large an arrangement as space may be at a premium, and ensure it is easy to water and keep fresh. You will need a bunch of mimosa, a bunch of daffodils and some garden greenery.

INGREDIENTS

A small basket, approximately 20cm × 15cm (8in × 6in)

Plastic bag or polythene

Half-block of green florist's foam

Flowers and foliage, see above

Scissors

Skewer or chopstick

❧

1 Line the basket with a plastic bag (unpunctured) or some polythene. Soak the foam well in water. Wedge the foam into the basket, so that it is held in place. Using a selection of greenery, place some sprigs all the way around the basket and across the top so that the foam is completely covered.

2 *Cut the mimosa into small sprigs about 12mm (½in) longer than the greenery, and place them into the arrangement. Any light, fluffy plant material, such as gypsophila, could be substituted for the mimosa.*

3 *To place the daffodils into the arrangement cut each one as you come to it, allowing about 2·5cm (1in) to go into* *the foam. Daffodil stalks do not respond well to being pushed into foam, so make a hole first with a skewer or* *chopstick and then place the daffodil into the hole.*

Edged basket & Floral clock

Both these gifts are easy to make but look very professional. The basket of soaps would look stunning in a bathroom, while the pressed flower clock adds a pretty country touch to a kitchen or bedroom.

$\mathscr{E}$dged basket

This edged basket would make a wonderful bathroom or cloakroom decoration; as an alternative to putting soaps in the centre you could fill it with bath cubes or pot pourri. If you wanted to give the basket as a hostess gift then it could be filled with sweets or chocolates. You will need a hot glue gun as using this is much easier than trying to wire the ingredients onto the basket. This basket used some Spanish moss, 15 sticks of cinnamon, 25 nutmegs, 25 slices of dried orange, half a bunch of nigella seed heads and 2 bunches of Evelien roses.

INGREDIENTS

Flowers, foliage, fruit and spices, see above

Glue gun and glue

A shallow basket with no handle, approximately 22·5–25cm (9–10in) in diameter

A reel of silver rose wire

Scissors

Tissue paper or paper doily

Contents for basket

ð

1 Make the Spanish moss into a sausage shape. Put some glue around the top edge of the basket and place the moss sausage over the glue. Press down, taking care not to burn yourself. Once the glue has cooled, use some reel wire to bind the moss onto the basket in a few strategic points to tame it and make the moss a similar height all around the basket. Glue on the cinnamon sticks in threes.

150

2 *Glue the nutmegs onto the piles of cinnamon and then add the orange slices, some whole and some in halves and quarters. Other citrus fruits could be used, such as grapefruit or lemons or some dried apple. Then cut the heads from the nigella and glue them to the basket between the bundles of cinnamon.*

3 *Cut the roses quite short and glue them to the basket between the nigella seed heads. Line the basket with a little tissue paper or a paper doily and then fill the basket with pretty guest soaps, pot pourri, sweets or chocolates.*

$\mathcal{F}$loral clock

Using pressed flowers to decorate a clock makes your gift a little more personal. But, before you buy your clock, check with the store that the clock will come to pieces, or it could be disastrous! You will need a selection of pressed flowers and leaves in complementary colours and of a similar size. I have used ballerina roses, pink larkspur and rue leaves with some small pieces of yellow solidago flowers.

INGREDIENTS

Clock with removable glass

Pressed flowers and leaves, see above

Tweezers

Tapestry needle

Latex adhesive

1 Play around with the leaves and flowers at first to see what type of design you would like to do. Use tweezers so as not to damage the plant material. Once you are happy with your ideas, you can start to glue down the design. Begin with the leaves as they form the backbone of the design.

2 *Using the tapestry needle, apply a small blob of latex adhesive to each leaf. Do not put too much on at once or it may seep out. Here the leaves have been glued on in a circular design. Next add small pieces of solidago between each leaf.*

3 *Make sure each flower is well glued before proceeding with the next ingredient. Lastly add the roses and the* pink larkspur. *If you have put too much adhesive behind the flowers, carefully clean it off the clock face.* Then polish the glass and re-assemble the clock.

Pot pourri

Homemade pot pourri is far superior to the mass-produced, scented wood-shaving collections usually found in the shops. You can grow or harvest all manner of natural plants and pods for your mixtures, and long-lasting fragrances can be achieved using essential oils and orris root.

Pot pourri

This selection of four different pot pourris representing the four seasons would make a wonderfully different gift at a very reasonable cost. Drying flowers and leaves for pot pourri can easily be done in a microwave by laying the items on kitchen paper and cooking for a couple of minutes on medium to high heat. Although you lose some of the shape, the colour remains, together with any fragrance. You will need four differing sets of ingredients – *Spring*: 10 lemon slices, 1 cup dried green hellebores, 1 cup dried delphinium flowers and 1 cup any dried grey-green leaves; *Summer*: 1 cup dark pink larkspur flowers, 1½ cups ivy leaves, ½ cup cloves and 1 cup pink rose petals plus a few whole roses; *Autumn*: 10 dried apple slices, 10 dried orange slices, 1 cup tangerine-coloured rose petals and 1 cup mixed beech masts and peach stones; *Winter*: 1 cup conifer leaves, 1 cup costus flowers (small pine cones), 1 cup broken cinnamon, 1 cup red rose petals and a few whole roses.

INGREDIENTS

Pot pourri ingredients, see above

4 mixing bowls

30g (1oz) orris root

4 × 2·5ml bottles of essential or perfume oils

Metal spoon

4 plastic bags

4 elastic bands

4 suitable containers

Glue gun and glue

ଅ

1 Organize all your ingredients, making sure you have a sufficient amount to fill the four containers you have chosen. Mix the four ingredients for each season together in small bowls and add a quarter of the orris root to each one. Add the oil of your choice and mix well, using a metal spoon. Choose oils that reflect the ingredients used in the pot pourri, for example lemon oil for spring, and cinnamon for winter.

2 *Tip the mixture for each pot pourri into a separate plastic bag and shake well. Secure the tops with elastic bands and leave to mature for at least a week. The pot pourri mixtures can then be emptied into their respective containers.*

3 These plain containers are ideal for pot pourri. They are inexpensive and easy to decorate for a gift. Remove some of the larger pieces from each pot pourri and then arrange them in a pretty group on the corresponding lid. A glue gun is a quick and efficient way to fix them in position but other strong glues could be used instead.

Birthday sampler & Mother's Day basket

These delightful presents would be suitable for many occasions, other than those suggested. The striped design of the basket has a fresh modern feel to it, while the flower sampler is reminiscent of times gone by.

$\mathcal{B}$irthday sampler

This flower picture is intended to make one think of Victorian needlework and children's samplers. The time needed to make such beautiful works of art is quite incredible. The pressed flower version, although still a fairly fiddly project, takes considerably less time and a little less patience. Alternative background materials could be used, such as linen or canvas, depending upon your particular taste. The pressed flowers needed for this project are 3 ivy leaves, 7 small fern leaves, 5 pieces of alyssum, 7 sprays of freesia, 3 pieces of alchemilla and a selection of pansies, roses, potentillas and astrantias. Finally, you will also need a large number of potentilla centres – about 12 per letter.

INGREDIENTS

Wooden frame, approximately 30cm × 25cm (12in × 10in), with glass and hardboard back

Piece of 3mm (⅛in) thick foam, approximately 30cm × 25cm (12in × 10in)

Piece of calico, approximately 30cm × 25cm (12in × 10in)

Tweezers

Fabric glue

Flowers and foliage, see above

Large tapestry needle
☙

1 Place the back of the frame on the table and cover with the piece of foam. Lay the calico on top of the foam. Using tweezers to lift the flowers, here potentillas, arrange the layout of the name that you want to spell, placing it either diagonally across the picture or horizontally across the middle. Once you are satisfied with the position of the name and shape of the letters, glue down the potentilla middles. Hold each flower with tweezers, then apply a dab of glue with a tapestry needle.

2 Arrange the plant material in the bottom corner of the picture, by placing the ivy leaves on first and then adding the freesia sprays between the leaves. Place the pale alyssum against the dark ivy leaves for contrast. Add the larger flowers next and then the smaller ones like potentilla.

3 Then arrange the top corner of the sampler, again starting with the leaves to obtain the right outline shape. Place the

smaller bits of alchemilla between the ferns. Then mix the pansies and roses together in the centre of the design.

Finally glue all the flowers firmly into position, applying the glue with the needle, and frame the picture.

ℳother's Day basket

Although this flower basket is very different to the style of flower arranging we are all used to, its graphic design with stripes crossing the basket is fun to experiment with. You can easily vary the stripes by changing the colour of the contents or shape of the basket. You will need 4 or 5 hydrangea heads, 30 wired cream helichrysum, 24 heads of cream carthamus, a bunch of pink larkspur and 8 pink peonies.

INGREDIENTS

Long shallow basket

3 blocks of dried flower foam

Flowers, see above

ะเ

1 Fill the basket with the dried flower foam and wedge the last piece in to make sure the foam does not move. Start the arrangement with the peonies and place a straight row beneath the handle in the centre of the basket. You will need to have very short stems on all the ingredients.

3 Complete the remaining side of the basket like the first, with bands of larkspur, carthamus, helichrysum and finally hydrangea. Insert these so that they overlap the basket slightly to soften the edges.

2 You can either build up the stripes in the arrangement from the centre outwards, working on both sides at once or complete one side of the basket at a time. Move on to the next ingredient, the larkspur. Break the bunch into short pieces about 7·5–10cm (3–4in) long. Place a band of these next to the peonies. Then put 12 heads of carthamus next to the larkspur. Next make a row of 15 helichrysum, and follow this with a final strip made from pieces of hydrangea.

Teddy bear ring

This enchanting ring would make a suitable gift for a young person or someone who is simply young at heart. The colours can be changed to suit the tastes of the recipient but any combination would be equally charming.

Teddy bear ring

This lovely little teddy bear ring would make a special gift for the little girl in your life and possibly for some bigger girls as well! Teddies are a perennial favourite and, although flock-covered bears have been used here, a small fluffy bear would also look adorable. You could make this ring with fresh flowers but it would not last for long; this combination of dried and preserved materials will last well if hung out of strong light. To make the ring, you will need a bunch of pale pink larkspur, some sprays of canella berries, half a bunch of green carthamus and some preserved foliage.

INGREDIENTS

Scissors

Flowers and foliage, see above

Glue gun and glue

Twiggy wreath, approximately 20cm (8in) in diameter

Mother bear and two baby bears

1 Trim the foliage into small sprigs and glue it around the wreath. Arrange the sprigs so that some leaves face into the centre of the ring as well as facing outwards. Next, glue on some preserved foliage around the ring.

2 *Glue the teddy bears firmly into position, and hold them in place until the glue has cooled completely. Add in the heads from the bunch of carthamus. This is a very versatile dried ingredient as it has a good shape and fills arrangements well.*

3 *Then break the pink larkspur into small pieces and attach them around the whole wreath. Finally, fill any gaps with some small sprays of the canella berries.*

Wedding spoon

Spoons have been considered tokens of love and luck for many generations. A decorated wooden spoon makes an attractive good luck token for a bride. Alternatively, by using less flowers and including spices and fruit, a spoon would look lovely in a kitchen.

$\mathcal{W}$edding spoon

Wooden spoons, such as the beautifully carved Welsh love spoons, are a traditional gift for a bride. Decorating a spoon with flowers is quicker and easier than carving one, and provides a lovely way to show your affection and wish good luck to the recipient. Although these floral spoons were primarily designed as a bridal gift, they could also make a lovely birthday or Mother's day present or good luck gift. To make a similar wedding spoon, you will need a few flowers and pieces of foliage – flowers from the garden would be fine or use a few leftovers from an arrangement.

INGREDIENTS

Drill

Large wooden spoon

Approximately 2m (80in) ribbon, depending upon desired length

Glue

Small green frog (attachment for use with florist's foam)

Scissors

Tiny cube of green florist's foam

Flowers and foliage, see above

🦢

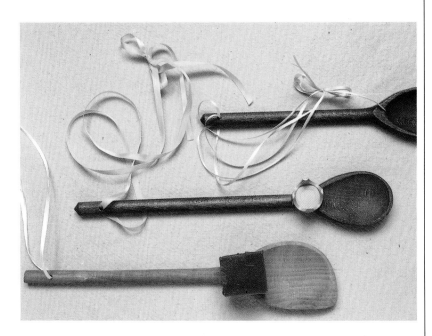

1 Drill a hole in the top of the handle of the spoon, either from front to back or from side to side, making sure it is large enough to take your choice of ribbon. Thread the ribbon through the hole and tie it into a firm bow. Glue the green frog onto the junction of the handle and the bowl of the spoon. Trim the prongs of the frog to make it

a little smaller. Impale a cube of foam, soaked in water, onto the frog.

2 *Cover the foam well with some pieces of greenery; unusual bits and pieces such as catkins look lovely. Allow the foliage to trail over the spoon handle and bowl in a random fashion.*

3 *Add in some flowers. You will need to trim the stems to about 5–7·5cm (2–3in). Here I've used a small number of* spray carnations. Try to choose flowers that last fairly well out of water. Wild flowers never last well and look much nicer left in the hedgerows, but many garden flowers would be suitable.

Preparing flowers for gifts

Packaging is a very important part of making your own gifts. A pretty box or ribbon, some cellophane or a special container can raise a homemade display into a special handmade creation! If you spend a little extra time planning the presentation of your gift, your efforts will be amply rewarded by the appreciative comments when you hand over the present.

Collecting various items in advance is well worth doing. I have a deep drawer that is full of bits and pieces that may well be just what I'm looking for – one day! Seriously, though, a collection of boxes or ribbons, pretty paper and string, and other odds and ends can make present manufacturing much easier.

CARE OF FRESH FLOWERS

If you are planning to give a gift of fresh flowers, it is obviously important to have the best quality flowers that have been treated to last as long as possible. If you grow flowers for cutting in your garden, then these should be fresh and with proper conditioning should last well. Good quality flowers from a florist can last even longer as they are often grown to be long lasting. It is important to have a good source for your flowers as half-dead flowers will never make a good arrangement and your time will not have been used to its best advantage.

Once you get your flowers indoors, whether they are home-grown or from a florist, cut the bottom of the stalks at an angle and immerse the flowers in deep water overnight. This should give them a good long drink which should help them to last longer in your arrangements.

DRYING FLOWERS

Many flowers will dry just as well at home as in commercial drying kilns. Producing an arrangement that you have grown and dried yourself is very satisfying.

Collect the flowers you wish to dry on a bright, dry day and harvest them just before they reach their full maturity. Strip off some of the lower leaves and tie in small bunches, fixing them with a strong elastic band. It is important not to use string for this purpose as the stems shrink during the drying process and the bunch may fall and damage some of your precious blooms!

Hang these small bunches somewhere warm and dark, but with reasonable air circulation. A dry loft or attic can be ideal – a garage is not suitable as the night temperatures may be too low to be beneficial to the flowers. A spare bedroom or cupboard with the doors ajar can sometimes be a solution. Once the flowers are dry, they can be stored in boxes packed with tissue paper and kept at a reasonable temperature.

PRESSING FLOWERS

Preserving flowers in a press is an easy technique if all the basic pointers are followed. Many people use presses (often unsuccessfully) as children, but good pressing is only possible if a few basic rules are followed.

• Only collect perfect specimens that have begun to open that day – and only pick on a bright, dry day, preferably in the morning.

• Choose mainly thin or flat flowers, such as pansies, larkspur and lawn daisies, and avoid thick, lumpy specimens such as chrysanthemums and thick-centred daisies.

• Use clean, dry blotting paper and pads of dry newspaper in your press. Place a pad of newspaper at the bottom of the press and cover with a sheet of blotting paper. Lay a few flowers on the blotting paper, making sure they do not touch or overlap and then cover them with more blotting paper. Continue building alternate layers of newspaper and blotting paper with flowers between, until you have reached a maximum of ten layers.

Screw down the press as firmly as possible and leave in a warm place for about six to eight weeks – without looking inside!

• Once your pressed flowers are ready to use, store them in a warm, dark place so that the petals don't fade and to prevent re-absorption of moisture, which would cause the flowers to turn mouldy. Cellophane-fronted paper bags or blotting paper folders work well for storage.

Fresh, dried and pressed flowers make lovely gifts. Collect baskets, ribbons and doilies in advance.

Wedding anniversaries

Flowers make the ideal gift for wedding anniversaries. For an especially thoughtful gift, you could incorporate an anniversary token into your posy or arrangement. Listed below are the traditional materials from which an anniversary gift should be made.

1st – Paper	9th – Pottery or willow	25th – Silver
2nd – Cotton	10th – Tin	30th – Pearl
3rd – Leather	11th – Steel	35th – Coral
4th – Fruit or flowers	12th – Silk or linen	40th – Ruby
5th – Wood	13th – Lace	45th – Sapphire
6th – Sugar or iron	14th – Ivory	50th – Gold
7th – Wool or copper	15th – Crystal	55th – Emerald
8th – Pottery or bronze	20th – China	60th – Diamond

Suppliers

For details of dried flowers, craft ingredients, and pressed flower ingredients and oils by mail order; also two-day craft courses on flowers and other crafts:

Joanna Sheen Limited
PO Box 52
Newton Abbot
Devon TQ12 4QH

For pot pourri ingredients and oils, and details of shops throughout the country:

Culpeper Limited
21 Bruton Street
London W1X 7DA

For details of dried flowers by mail order and farm shop:

Caroline Alexander
The Hop Shop
Castle Farm
Shoreham
Sevenoaks
Kent TN14 7UB

Index

ACKNOWLEDGEMENTS

Merehurst would like to thank the following for lending props for the photographs in this book: David Robertson and Peta Weston for creating the special backgrounds; Shirley Dupree for lending the wooden toys from her collection; and Margaret Check, Hazel Hurst and Nesta MacDonald who kindly lent their lace, table linen and crockery.